GUITAR WORLD Presents STEVE VAI's GUITAR WORKOUT

ISBN 978-1-4803-4440-2

HAL•LEONARD® CORPORATION

7777 W. BLUEMOUND RD. P.O. BOX 13819 MILWAUKEE, WI 53213

In Australia Contact:
Hal Leonard Australia Pty. Ltd.
4 Lentara Court
Cheltenham, Victoria, 3192 Australia
Email: ausadmin@halleonard.com.au

Cover photo by Chris Schwegler/ATLASICONS.COM

Visit Hal Leonard Online at
www.halleonard.com

CONTENTS

10-HOUR GUITAR WORKOUT

Since its appearance in *Guitar World* in 1990, Vai's intensive guitar regimen has been the Holy Grail for serious players. Here is the lesson that shaped a generation of guitarists.

Steve Vai sat down with guitarist/transcriber Dave Whitehill and outlined his practice routine for the January 1990 issue of *Guitar World*. Never before had a guitarist given such an in-depth explanation of his musical exercise regimen. It became a must-have for guitarists. Many of the players interviewed in GW have cited it as an influence on their development as guitarists. Here's a chance to experience the workout in its original form and to learn some of the things Vai has done to develop his formidable chops and remarkable music vocabulary.

To start, Vai presents the general philosophy behind his approach to the guitar. "I could sit here and tell you, 'Rule of thumb: try to always play clean,' or 'Rule of thumb: think melody.' But I wouldn't because I really don't think there are too many rules of thumb. If you try to do something that somebody else says is a rule of thumb, you might be going against your better judgment. Most of the time, innovation happens when people break the rules.

"A rule of thumb I could offer is: never take what anybody tells you as gospel. Music is an art form; it's an expression of yourself, and you have to do it the way your inner inclinations guide you. I'm not necessarily saying to do away with what anybody else may have to say either, because inspiration can come in many different forms. It can be useful to pick up tips from others through private lessons, magazine, records, the internet, etc. that can help build your own technique. You may discover certain exercises in this book that I did that I thought were helpful, but you shouldn't get carried away with what I or anyone else does, because you'll start sounding like the next guy and lose sight of your own musical identity.

"I could say, 'Play from the heart,' but what does that mean? It's easy to say and to intellectualize, but it's another thing to know it on an experiential level. 'Play from the heart' may mean, 'Play from your own heart,' or to simplify it, play whatever makes you the most content. You have the right to thoroughly enjoy what you play."

On his way to becoming a guitar virtuoso, Vai would practice 10 hours per day and document everything he did. The first hour was devoted to technical exercises, the second to scales and the third to some "chord thing." He'd repeat these areas three times and devote the remaining time to a "Sensitivity Hour," during which he would try to reproduce spoken phrases as passages on the guitar. In addition, the exercises were divided into three categories: linear picking, stretching, and angular. All of them are outlined in the following text.

LINEAR PICKING EXERCISES

To develop a strong, fluent alternate (down-up) picking technique, Vai recommends practicing "things that are technically awkward, like picking three or four notes on a string and crossing over to the next string and doing it again. Start very slowly and use a metronome; go all the way up and down the neck. Once you feel comfortable playing a certain pattern, set the metronome a little faster. Keep doing this and eventually, after several months, you're just wailing."

The first example of this type of linear exercise is based on an ascending pattern we'll simply call "1-2-3-4," as this refers to the order in which the fret-hand fingers are placed on each string (FIGURE 1). When playing this exercise, try to keep your fretting hand fingers as close as possible to the fingerboard. You should keep your first finger on the string until the fourth finger makes contact, at which point the first finger moves over to the next string. This is a great, uncomplicated exercise for a novice guitarist.

FIGURE 1

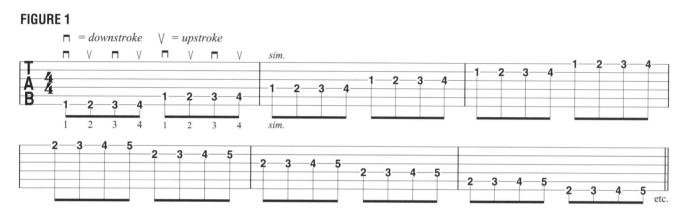

Vai then demonstrates an alternating variation (FIGURE 2) in which the fingering pattern (represented numerically below the tablature) follows the repeating sequence 1-2-3-4, 2-3-4-1, 3-4-1-2, 4-1-2-3. This alternating idea is also played on a single string (FIGURE 3) and has the added benefit of offering a great exercise in position shifting. The next step is to exhaust all other permutations of the 1-2-3-4 or any other four-note combination you find awkward and practice them in a similar manner.

FIGURE 2

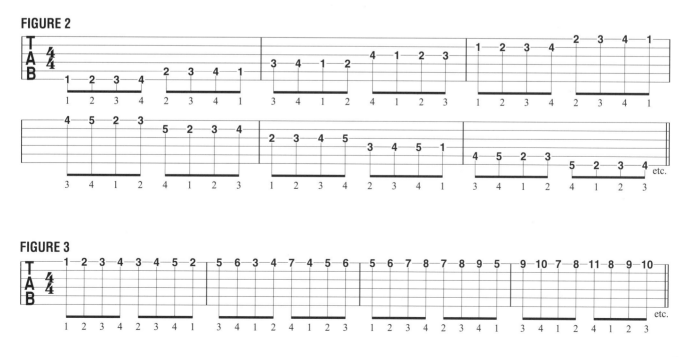

FIGURE 3

If we apply Vai's pragmatic approach to three-note-per-string combinations—for example, 1-3-4—the result would be the three exercises shown in FIGURES 4-6. These exercises present a workout for the brain as well as the fingers. Approach them slowly at first, until the logic behind each pattern sinks in.

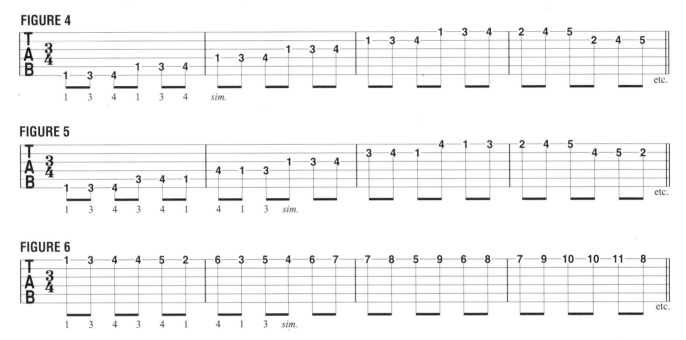

FIGURE 4

FIGURE 5

FIGURE 6

Of course, two-note-per-string patterns could also be used for linear picking exercises (FIGURES 7 and 8). If you have problems crossing strings with the same finger, you'll find the exercise shown in FIGURE 7 to be particularly beneficial. Roll your fretting finger over the strings as you switch from one to the next to keep the notes from "bleeding" or ringing into each other. To do this, simply straighten your first knuckle as you shift the fingertip pressure over to the next string.

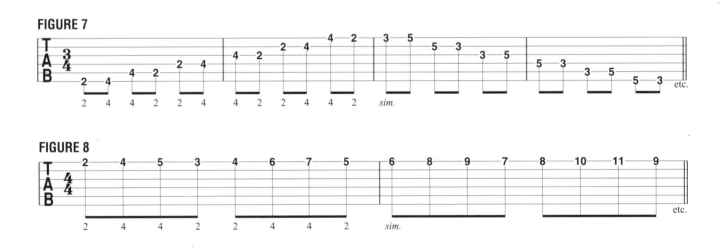

FIGURE 7

FIGURE 8

STRETCHING EXERCISES

The stretching exercises depicted in FIGURES 9 and 10 are played just like the two-note-per-string picking exercises, but here you want to gradually increase the span of your fretting hand. FIGURE 9 stretches each adjacent finger pair (1-2, 2-3, and 3-4). If you find it difficult to play any of these stretches in first position, begin higher up the neck and work your way down as your fingers become more limber and their range of motion increases.

Despite the awkward stretches, strive for clean execution and allow each note its full duration. If there's a big gap of silence between each note, you're cheating.

FIGURE 9

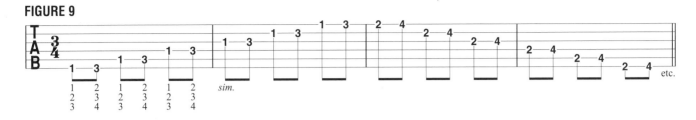

FIGURE 10 works the 1-3 and 2-4 finger pairs. In addition to these two exercises, try spanning four or five frets with the first and fourth fingers. As before, if you encounter any difficulty, begin higher up the neck until your hand muscles and ligaments become more flexible. Unlike weight lifting, "No pain, no gain" does not apply here. Stop if you feel any discomfort.

FIGURE 10

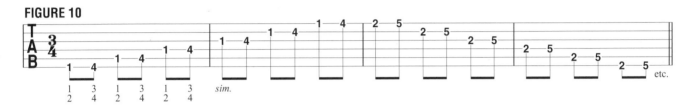

"Hand position is critical in all these exercises," Vai emphasizes. "Don't hook your thumb over the top of the neck. This will greatly decrease your stretching ability. Keep it centered behind the neck and your fingers parallel to the frets before you attempt a stretch."

ANGULAR EXERCISES

"Angular exercises improve your string-crossing chops," Vai says. "The more adept you are at crossing strings with the pick, the better your picking technique." FIGURE 11 exemplifies what angular exercises are all about. The general idea is to take a finger pattern, in this case 4-3-2-1, and work it across the strings, assigning one finger per fret. Since there are only three groups of four adjacent strings (first through fourth, second through fifth, and third through sixth), the entire pattern doesn't manifest itself until it is played on one of these three string groups.

FIGURE 11

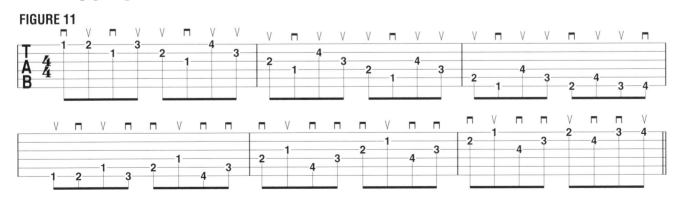

You may find it helpful to visualize three "phantom strings" on either side of the neck, to give you a reference for fingering the first six and last six notes of the exercise. With this approach, the progression of notes seems very natural. For example, when playing the first note (F) with the first finger (1), think in terms of the complete 4-3-2-1 pattern with the other fingers (2-3-4) on the imaginary strings. Therefore, only the first finger is being used. As the pattern moves across the strings, all four fingers are eventually brought into play. Likewise, as you run out of strings in bar 3, all fingers, except the fourth, move off the neck onto the imaginary strings.

FIGURE 12 shows a 1-2-3-4 applied to an angular exercise. Use the imaginary strings approach to make it easier to figure out the corresponding exercises for other finger patterns. For example, an angular exercise based on a 1-3-2-4 finger pattern would begin 4, 2-4, 3-2-4, 1-3-2-4, as illustrated in the first bar of FIGURE 13.

FIGURE 12

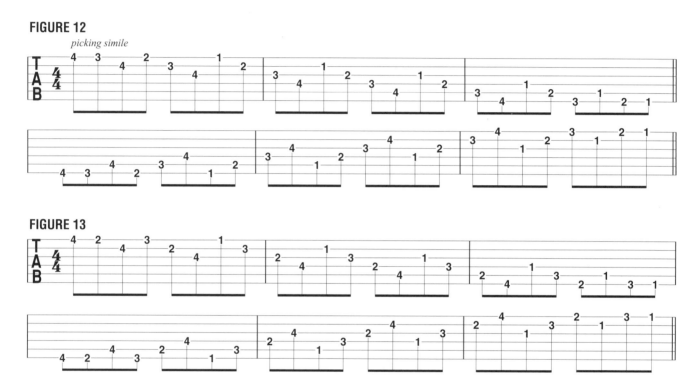

FIGURE 13

CHORD STUDIES

Vai's three one-hour chord-study sessions were as varied as the other areas of his workout. "For the first hour, I'd study charts. I'd take *The Real Book* (an anthology of jazz and fusion standards used for decades by jazz musicians and students, particularly at the Berklee College of Music in Boston) and play stuff like the Hammerstein/Kern standard 'The Last Time I Saw Paris'." He would spend the second hour experimenting with unusual chords and voicings, and "for the third hour, I would just jam on a rhythm like a funky Em11 chord vamp. Once I got a groove going with it, I'd record it and solo over it. I would also invert and arpeggiate different types of chords, like Gmaj7."

FIGURE 14

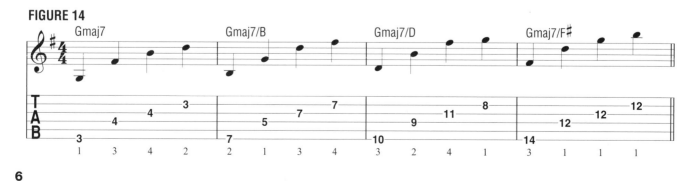

"Invert" and "arpeggiate" require some explanation. "Inversion" is a technique in which a chord is voiced so that any of its notes other than the root is the lowest (bass) note. In FIGURE 14, a Gmaj7 chord (G B D F♯) is voiced first with the root in the bass (bar 1), then the third, fifth, and seventh. "Arpeggiation" means playing the notes of a chord in succession rather than simultaneously. Other common four-note chords, such as the sixth, dominant seventh, minor seventh, and minor sixth, are given the same treatment in FIGURES 15–18. Try to identify any familiar chord shapes (or fragments of them) as you move through these inversions. For example, in FIGURE 16, it's easy to visualize the G7 barre chord shape in bar 1 and an A-shaped barre chord in bar 4.

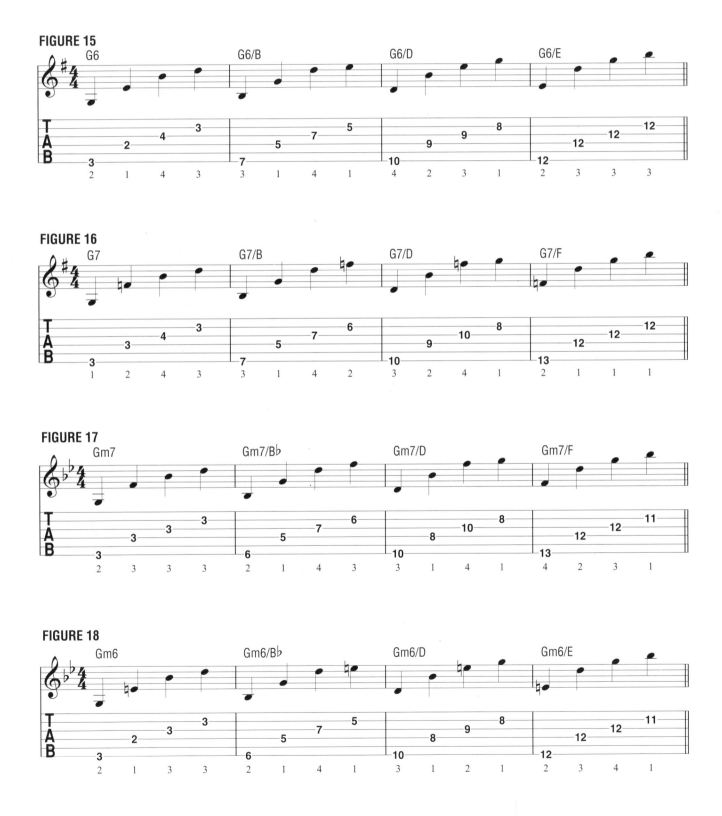

SCALE/MODE STUDIES

Vai's scale workout involves playing the major scale in all 12 keys at 10 different tempos, and practicing scales in interval patterns. For example, after playing the G major scale in FIGURE 19—a standard scale shape that all novice guitarists should learn—he plays it in thirds (FIGURE 20), fourths (FIGURE 21), and fifths (FIGURE 22). Practicing scales in interval patterns like this is an excellent way to improve your coordination and come up with alternatives to playing straight ascending and descending linear patterns in your lead playing, which can quickly become boring.

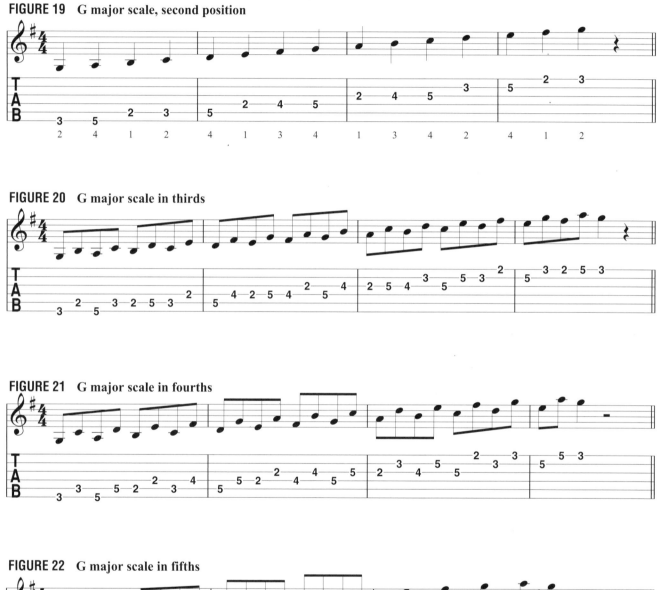

FIGURE 19   G major scale, second position

FIGURE 20   G major scale in thirds

FIGURE 21   G major scale in fourths

FIGURE 22   G major scale in fifths

Vai then runs through all the diatonic modes in thirds (FIGURES 23–28). The guitarist advises, "Play them slowly to make sure they're perfect—clean, even, and right in sync with the metronome—and concentrate on making sure your pick isn't moving that much."

FIGURE 23 G Dorian mode in thirds, second position w/first-finger stretch

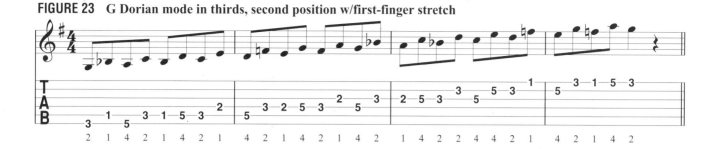

FIGURE 24 G Phrygian mode in thirds, third position

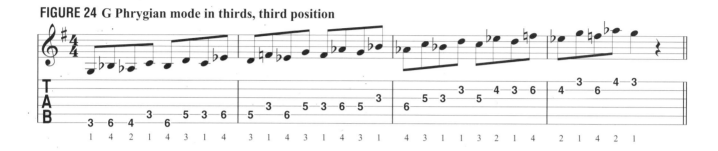

FIGURE 25 G Lydian mode in thirds, second position

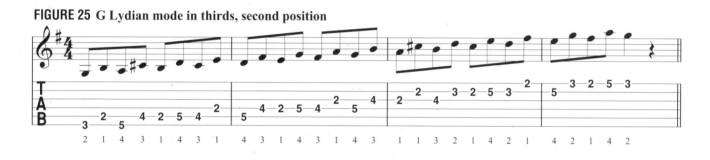

FIGURE 26 G Mixolydian mode in thirds, second position

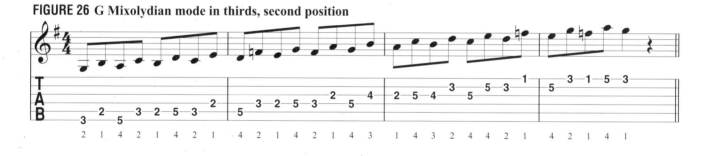

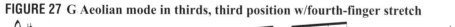

FIGURE 27 G Aeolian mode in thirds, third position w/fourth-finger stretch

FIGURE 28 G Locrian mode, third position

Vai says his woodshedding experience while studying at Berklee "was very mechanical. I used to try and balance the technical with the emotional in my playing and found that, once I got my motor skills sharpened, it became a lot easier for me to express myself, as long as I didn't get carried away with my chops. It's very easy to say to yourself, 'Wow, I've got chops now,' as a result of all these mechanical-type exercises, but then you'll lose sight of why you have the chops in the first place."

In terms of ear training, it's very helpful and educational when practicing modes to have a bass note "drone" sounding the root note (G in these examples). This way you can really hear and internalize the mood each mode creates. Without the root note of the mode in your ear, the brain will just pick up on the relative major scale from which the mode is derived. For example, when playing G Phrygian (FIGURE 24), it's easy to gravitate toward hearing it as being an E♭ major scale starting on G.

The Lydian mode (FIGURE 25) is one of Vai's favorite scales. The raised, or "sharped," fourth in this pattern gives the Lydian mode its distinctive, exotically beautiful quality. Play this pattern with a friend strumming a G chord, and you should notice a definite Vai sound.

Asked whether he used the other possible positions for the major scale, Vai responds, "No, I just used to play in that one position; the others were useless to me. The only reason I used those scales was to get the sound of them in my head and get my fingers going. I didn't want to learn scales in a million different positions because I was afraid my playing would become too position-oriented. I used to do this really cool exercise in every key: starting with E major, I would go from the lowest to the highest note [plays FIGURE 29] and then come back down."

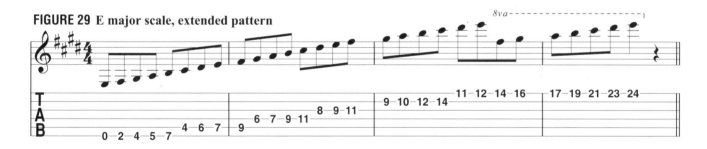

FIGURE 29 E major scale, extended pattern

You'll have to figure out your own fingering for this elongated scale pattern. It comes down to whatever works for you. Experiment with finger slides and quick, stealthy position shifts. Bearing in mind that the idea is to minimize hand movement wherever possible, moving your first finger frantically from note to note doesn't make much sense... unless you're going for a sitar-like vibe. Vai says, "The premise is that you have to do it by ear and play it differently each time without making a mistake, otherwise you have to start over. Your fingers will kind of develop 'eyes,' and you'll get a feel for playing the scale you're hearing in your head instead of being absorbed by the mechanics of it all."

LEAVING THE WOODSHED FOR OTHER REALMS

"Anyway, that's about nine hours of practice, and that was just on the first day. On the second day, I'd do less but move onto other things. I'd devote three hours to the mechanics, then work on vibrato, or take hammer-ons, pull-offs and 'flutters' [trills] and work on those for an hour." That may sound rather ambitious, but Vai also makes time for working on the feel of his playing. "I would always reserve the last hour of my routine for just soloing and jamming. You know, just feeling it, forgetting everything and just doing it.

"Later, I used to do this thing called the 'Sensitivity Hour,' where I'd try to play with as much extreme sensitivity as I could. I would record a chord progression, like this [plays FIGURE 30a] then think of a phrase in my head—like a word or a sentence—and try to play it melodically on the guitar."

FIGURE 30a

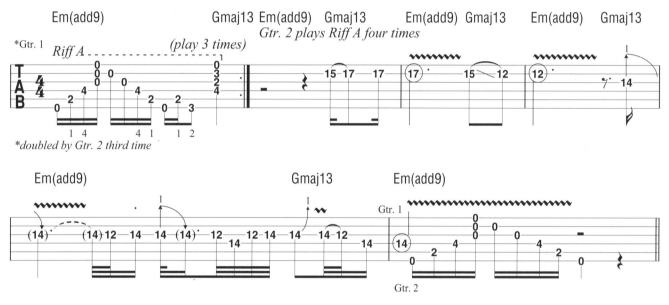

To illustrate his point further, Vai asks Whitehill to say a word or a sentence. Whitehill reflects on the solo Vai had just played in FIGURE 30a, and replies, "Hey, Steve, that was really nice!" Vai then mimics this sentence in the first two bars of FIGURE 30b, following up with variations in each of the subsequent phrases. Each note corresponds to a syllable, and the rhythms follow the natural speech pattern.

FIGURE 30b

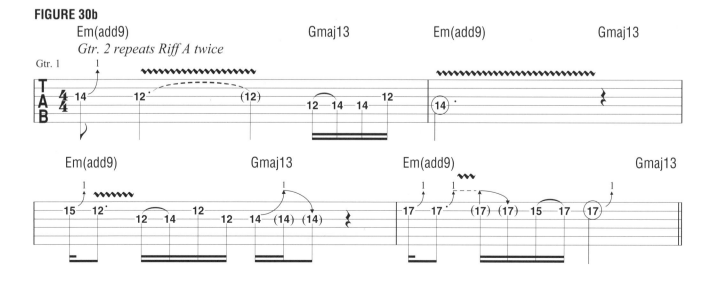

Vai explains: "You can start speaking your mind to yourself. Some people do this, and this is the way they pray—they pray to themselves when they play the instrument. It's very expressive and a lot better than thinking, OK, I'm in the key of E minor and this [plays the second chord of the progression, Gmaj13] is probably a Gmaj6 or a major seventh with the 13th and ninth, and I can play these notes [plays the notes D, A, and E in descending fourths on the first, second, and third strings in the ninth position].

"It's much easier to just say something to yourself. What happens then is that you start saying things that are extremely personal, that probably only you can understand, but the personality behind each phrase will reach your audience. It'll make your solo mean something very special and it'll add a certain feel to the way you play it. This technique can be very useful for pulling yourself out of a creative rut. Of course, your frame of mind will be dictated by the rhythm. It's tricky and requires discipline, but it's worth trying because it's so expressive."

Examples of "talking guitar" in Vai's discography include songs such as "Yankee Rose" with David Lee Roth and "The Dangerous Kitchen" with Frank Zappa. "It all started with Zappa's 'The Jazz Discharge Party Hat,'"

Vai reveals. "Frank had this half-talking/half-singing thing he used to do. It made me realize that everything you do and say has a pitch that can be translated into music. If you take our conversation right now and put a metronome to it and stop the tape on every syllable you will find... that there are notes... to everything you say. Take those phrases and write them down in notation while trying to capture the right inflections. It's extremely time consuming, because it's really tough to get every little nuance of talking onto manuscript paper. But you can even go so far as to orchestrate it."

TRANSCRIBING

"I used to transcribe everything from lead sheets, to guitar solos and drum parts, to band scores, to parts of orchestra scores for Frank, which was really hard to do, because acoustically, your ear can decipher only three or four different sounds at one time. You have to be able to focus and concentrate on one instrument among many. You can do this by adjusting the EQ, listening to the recording in mono, using phase cancellation to hear certain things, listening to just one side in mono, or flipping the channels over [reversing the speaker wiring or headphone placement] because you hear things differently in each ear.

"Listening to things at half-speed helps tremendously. It's really weird; sometimes you hear things at half-speed that you never would've thought were on the recording. Using a different tape deck will change the sound, too. You might find one deck is better for pulling the bottom out and the other is good for hearing the top end."

In closing, Vai says, "Transcribing is a form of meditation. When I was doing it, I was so enthralled with it and the idea of working for Zappa that I would spend literally 12 hours a day doing nothing but transcribing. Sometimes, when you're listening to a short snippet of music over and over, it sends you off into another world. When you concentrate on one thing for long enough, your awareness can become totally absorbed in the moment of it. It's an exercise in being alert and present."

REPRINTED FROM *GUITAR WORLD*, APRIL 2004

30-HOUR GUITAR WORKOUT

by Steve Vai

In 1990, I sat down with *Guitar World* for an interview, from which my 10-Hour Guitar Workout was extracted. When *GW* recently asked me to revise the workout, I decided to rewrite the program entirely in order to incorporate more of the wisdom I've gathered over the years.

I must have accumulated a lot of "wisdom" in 14 years, because what I have responded with is my new 30-Hour Guitar Workout. Compared with its predecessor, this program provides a more complete overview of elements that may help to balance a player's focus and personal goals on the instrument.

From my experience, I've found there are, in general, three types of guitarists: casual players who may use the guitar solely as a vehicle to write songs or just to enjoy playing; working musicians who are relatively accomplished and dedicated to a life with the instrument; and players who are intensely driven and relentless in their pursuit to accomplish brilliant and unique things on the instrument by discovering their distinctive abilities and talents and, eventually, presenting them effortlessly, with no apparent bounds.

Chances are good you fit into the first or second profile I've described. In fact, if there is any question as to whether you should pursue the direction of the third profile, then my suggestion would be, do not try; that category is reserved for those who feel they have no choice but to be unique. There is no question in the mind of those players; true artists are compelled by their desires, and usually nothing can stop them.

Please note: I'm not implying that one of these groups is better than another or represents players who have a deeper love of music than those in the other groups. Where you may fit into one of these groups is totally relative to you as a player, and it's all good. I'm simply creating groups based on the desires and goals of distinct types of players, and I'll add that there are myriad blends of all these categories. Although the following workout is intended primarily for the third group of people, elements from the regimen may be incorporated into any daily practice routine. In that respect, any guitarist can benefit from aspects of the workout.

WORKOUT PHILOSOPHY

I've always believed that everyone has the ability to discover and cultivate his or her own unique voice on an instrument; doing so requires that one listen to one's inner voice and then find the courage to express it. To that end, the following lesson is not meant to steer students into sounding like someone else but to equip them with some of the tools that are essential to discovering their own voice, while simultaneously helping them become thoroughly balanced musical beings.

I should note that the workout is geared for people that love the challenge of a disciplined curriculum and truly want to master the instrument. The concept behind doing so is easy: start by playing something—a bend, a riff, a scale, a song—very slowly; if you make a mistake, start over; do this over and over, until you can play it flawlessly—and I do mean *flawlessly*—many times in a row. Next, gradually increase the tempo. Eventually you'll be flailing about like a madman.

This doesn't necessarily mean you will become a great or effective musician or songwriter, but it may mean you can develop a fierce technique. Being an inspired musician is a gift that can't necessarily be taught, and personal inspiration is an individual experiential thing; there are no words that can be written that can convey how to discover and listen to your unique inspiration. But the good news is you are probably doing it one way or another. If not, you can discover how to find your own unique inspiration by cultivating within yourself a passion for it.

BEFORE YOU BEGIN

Focus. This is the most important element in this program. The way you mentally approach this or any other exercise is more important than putting in the hours and going through the motions. It is tremendously important that you gear up mentally for practice, gig, rehearsal, songwriting—whatever you're going to do. Understand that the attitude and frame of mind you have when entering into a focused endeavor is one of the few things you do have within your power. Remember: *It's all in the mind!*

You can basically convince yourself of anything and make it happen. Your perspective and attitude will reflect in the quality of your achievements. Your real work in accomplishing anything is in cultivating a positive mental attitude towards your goals and actions.

The good news is you have the ability to do this by choosing the thoughts you decide to think. It may at first be difficult to identify and break old negative patterns of thinking, but if you stand guard of your thoughts it can be done. Choosing whatever thoughts you want to think is a freedom that can never be taken away and is the very thing that creates the situations and circumstances of your outer life. And it's your birthright and is free! What a great design.

OK, Now…

Tune your guitar. Never play out of tune unless for a desired effect, such as working on a quarter-tone scale... or playing with a desire to have an out-of-tune earthy type sound.

CATEGORIES

I've divided the 30-Hour Workout into eight categories:

1. Finger Exercises

2. Scales

3. Chords

4. Ear training

5. Sight-reading

6. Composing/songwriting

7. Music theories

8. Jamming

In addition, I've arranged these categories into three 10-hour-per-day sessions. Bear in mind that the amount of time and focus you put into the program will be directly reflected in your playing.

I feel these categories provide a good mix of the various elements that go into becoming a thoroughly rounded musician. Note, however, that I will only be outlining concepts here; it's up to you to research and discover more on your own. There are plenty of instructional books, CDs, and DVDs on the market, and many schools offer home-study courses that teach you all types of finger exercises, chords, scales, theory, and so on. In addition, guitar-related information is plentiful on the internet. Of course, I encourage you to explore other categories, ideas, and concepts not mentioned here. That's one of the great things about playing the guitar—there are essentially no rules, and a person's ability to be unique is only limited by their courage and imagination.

Although the following workout is geared toward a rock style of playing, you may want to substitute various elements that are more appropriate for the style of music you're interested in. If you decide you don't want to learn conventional things, you may choose to replace one or more of these categories with something you're more comfortable with. You'll have to come up with them, though.

One last note: When I was a young practicing musician, I would keep a log of all the time I spent on the instrument, with a specific breakdown of everything I did. I guess I was just anal that way. While this approach worked for me, it may not be for everybody. It does, however, help you to chart your progress.

HOURS 1, 11, AND 21: FINGER EXERCISES

Finger exercises are great for developing dexterity and control. When performing them, pace yourself with a metronome or drum machine and start very slowly. It might help to imagine how you want the notes to sound, then perform them over and over, until they sound exactly the way you hear them in your head. I used to do this, and it's a great way to gain control over your playing. I would also experiment with different pick positions, dynamics, and so on. Whatever you do, be sure to focus on *every single note* you play. I can't stress enough the importance of this.

There are literally thousands of finger exercises, and they can all help you achieve different objectives. In this workout, I'll explain the following categories of finger exercises:

- Linear
- Angular
- Hammer-ons and Pull-offs
- Alternate Fingers
- Tapping
- Sweeping
- Multiple Picking

I would advise you to tailor your exercises around the style you're most interested in. The idea is to find things that are awkward to play and then work on them slowly, until you can play them perfectly. Ultimately, you want your playing to be a reflection of what you hear in your head.

Linear Exercises

FIGURE 1 depicts a basic linear finger exercise. It follows an ascending pattern we'll simply call "1-2-3-4," as this refers to the order in which the fret-hand fingers (index, middle, ring, pinkie) are placed on each string (fret-hand fingerings are indicated below the tablature). FIGURE 2 presents an alternating variation on this drill. The fingering pattern follows the repeating sequence 1-2-3-4, 2-3-4-1, 3-4-1-2, 4-1-2-3. The alternating fingering idea can also be played on a single string, as demonstrated in FIGURE 3. I find this drill to be a great exercise in *position shifting*.

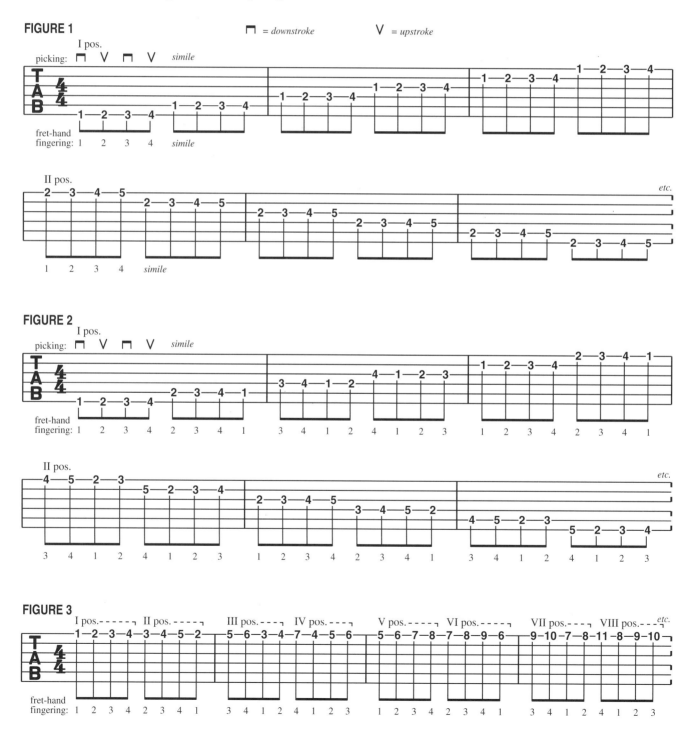

The next step is to exhaust all other permutations of the 1-2-3-4 combination, such as 4-3-2-1, 4-2-3-1, 1-3-2-4—whatever four-note sequence you find awkward—and practice them in a similar manner.

If we apply this fingering approach to three-note-per-string combinations, for example 1-3-4, the result would be the three exercises shown in **FIGURES 4–6**. Of course, two-note-per-string patterns could also be used for linear picking exercises, as demonstrated in **FIGURES 7** and **8**. The exercise shown in **FIGURE 7** will be beneficial to those of you who may have problems switching strings with the same fretting finger. Roll the finger over the strings as you switch from one to the next to keep the notes from bleeding (ringing) into each other.

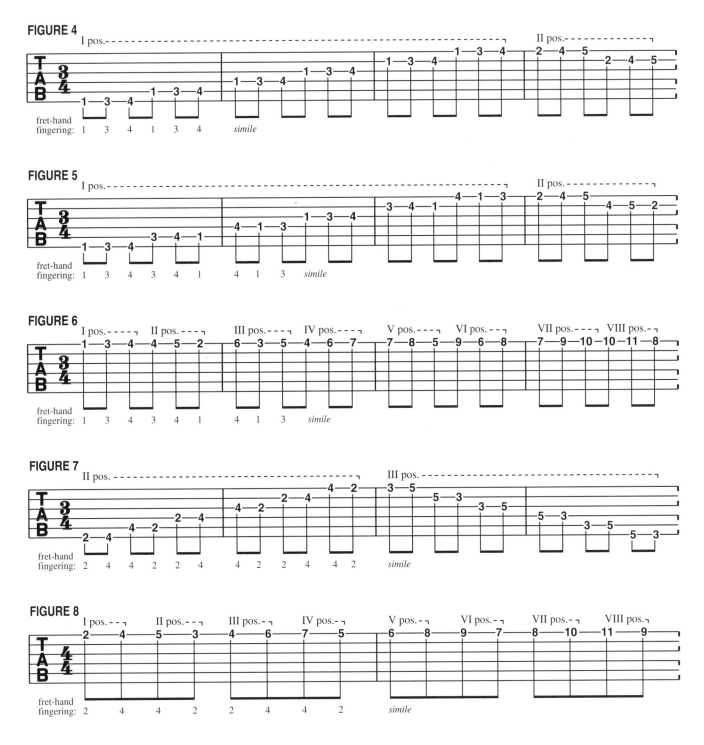

Angular Exercises

An effective way to improve your string-crossing technique is to perform what I call "angular" exercises. **FIGURE 9** exemplifies what I'm talking about. The general idea is to take a fingering pattern, in this case 4-3-2-1, and work it across the strings in a single position, assigning one finger per string and using *sweep* or *economy picking* (consecutive downstrokes or upstrokes on adjacent strings) wherever possible. I've included picking strokes above the tablature in this exercise to guide you. Each sweep (indicated by an upstroke or downstroke symbol followed by a broken horizontal line and a bracket) should be performed as a single pick stroke, with the pick being dragged across the strings in a continuous movement. Since there are only three groups of four adjacent strings (1–4, 2–5, and 3–6), the entire angular pattern doesn't manifest itself until it's played on one of these string groups.

FIGURE 9

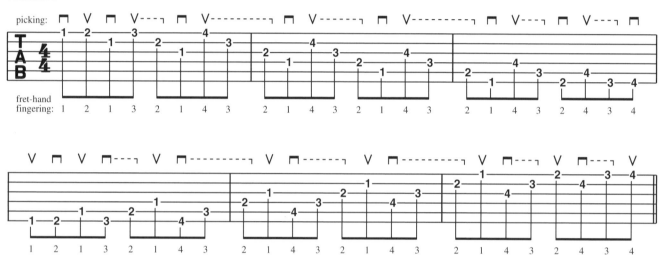

When performing **FIGURE 9**, I find it helpful to visualize three imaginary strings on either side of the neck, as this provides a point of reference for fingering the first six and last six notes of this exercise. With this approach, the progression of notes seems very natural. When I fret the first note (F) with my index finger, I'm thinking in terms of the complete 4-3-2-1 pattern, with the other three fingers (4-3-2) being on the imaginary strings. Thus, only the first finger is used. As the pattern moves across the strings, all four fingers are eventually brought into play. Likewise, as you run out of strings in bar 3, all fingers but the fourth move off the neck onto imaginary strings.

FIGURE 10 is an angular exercise based on a 1-2-3-4 fingering pattern. Again, I've included picking strokes and fret-hand fingerings above and below the tablature to guide you.

FIGURE 10

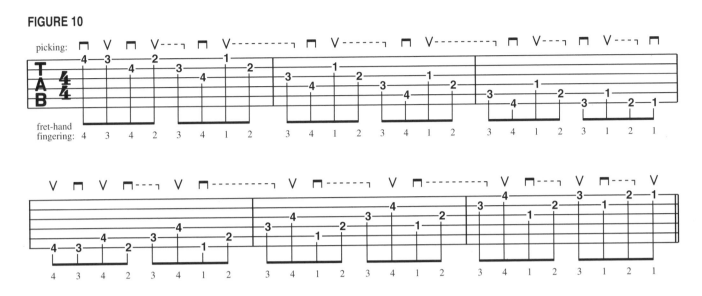

Using the "imaginary strings" approach should make it a little easier to devise exercises based on other fingering patterns. For example, an angular exercise based on a 1-3-2-4 fingering pattern would begin on the high E string and go 4, 2-4, 3-2-4, 1-3-2-4, as demonstrated in **FIGURE 11**.

FIGURE 11

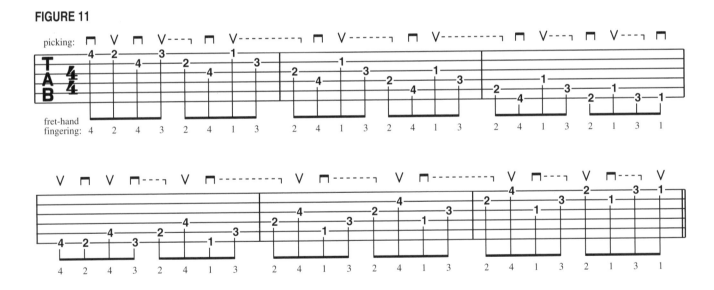

Allocate the first 30 minutes of your practice session to linear exercises and the next 30 minutes to angular exercises. Try to come up with your own exercises that suit your purposes and use them interchangeably. Due to the mathematical nature of these types of exercises, they're more easily worked out on paper than in your head (more on notating music later).

Hammer-ons and Pull-offs

The hammer-on is a technique whereby you pick a note (either fretted or open) and then sound a higher note on the same string by using one of your fretting fingers to tap the string like a hammer. The pull-off involves picking a note, then sounding a lower note (either fretted or open) on the same string by releasing the first note's fretting finger, pulling the string slightly in toward your palm as you let go of it in order to keep it vibrating.

Hammer-ons and pull-offs seem to happen naturally when playing single-note lines, but there are particularly effective ways to isolate and strengthen these techniques. One efficient way to do this is to practice performing *trills*. A trill is a rapid, continuous alternation between two notes on the same string, performed using hammer-ons and pull-offs in combination.

An effective way to isolate and perfect your hammer-on and pull-off techniques is to practice playing trills for an extended period of time, such as a minute. Begin by trilling between any two notes that are a half step (one fret) apart, using your fretting hand's index and middle fingers, as demonstrated in **FIGURE 12**. Now do the same thing, but add a fret between the two fingers (see **FIGURE 13**). The next step would be to increase the distance between the fingers by another fret, as shown in **FIGURE 14**.

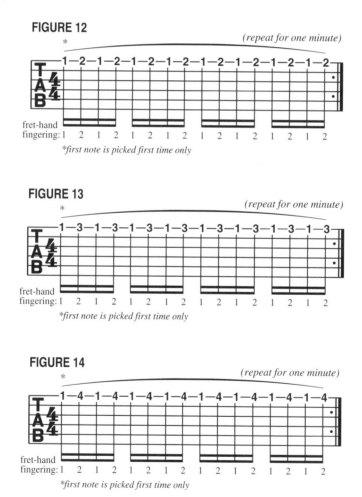

Now go back and play **FIGURES 12–14** again, this time using your index and ring fingers (1 and 3), then trill between your index finger and pinkie (1 and 4). Of course, you could exhaust all other finger combinations (2-3, 2-4, 3-4) and try to put as many frets between the fingers as possible (without hurting yourself!). Each time you go back to these trill drills, try adding some time to each exercise (maybe another 10 seconds or so).

Alternating Fingers

Try playing hammer-ons and pull-offs in various combinations, using different fingers, as in **FIGURES 15–17**. The goal in each case is to make all the notes sound even and clear and maintain a seamless *legato* feel.

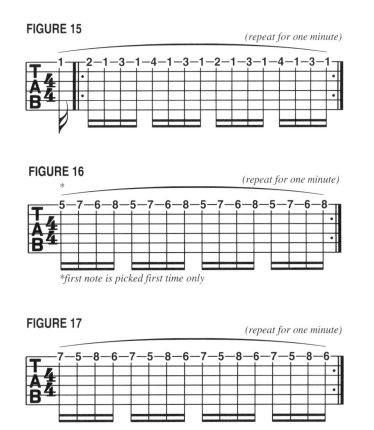

FIGURE 15

(repeat for one minute)

FIGURE 16

(repeat for one minute)

first note is picked first time only

FIGURE 17

(repeat for one minute)

Tapping

If you're interested in two-hand tapping, incorporate this into your hammer-on and pull-off practice time. The techniques are essentially the same for either hand, the only difference being that when you pull-off from a tapped note (a note hammered with one of the fingers of the picking hand), you flick the string slightly sideways, away from your chin. Use your imagination to create tapping techniques that suit your style, and try incorporating all the fingers of your picking hand on the neck.

FIGURES 18–20 are examples of tapping exercises to get you started. **FIGURE 18** is a simple drill designed to help you master the basic technique of tapping on one string, while **FIGURES 19** and **20** require that you cross strings, resulting in longer and more challenging patterns. In each of these latter two exercises, the key is to move the fingers of your fretting hand quickly from string to string in time to play the notes pulled off from the tapping finger cleanly.

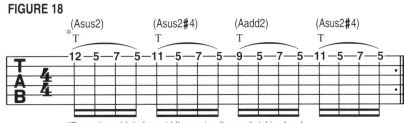

FIGURE 18

Tap string with index, middle, or ring finger of picking hand.

FIGURE 19

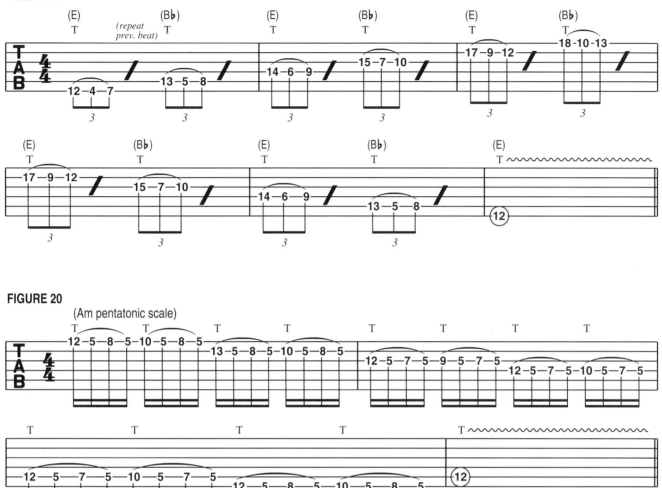

Sweep Picking

As stated earlier, sweep picking is a technique whereby you play one note and then another on an adjacent string in a single upstroke or downstroke. When learning to sweep pick you have to start very slowly and make sure you can hear every single note clearly (unless the effect you're going for is a sloppy one), then gradually bring the speed up. The key is to let go of each note with your fretting hand immediately after you've picked it in order to keep it from ringing into the next note. Create exercises that outline various chord shapes that you can sweep across. **FIGURES 21–23** are examples of sweep picking to get you started. You'll find that it's easier to sweep across an arpeggio shape and not have it sound like a strummed chord if you can finger each string individually with a different fingertip and avoid barring strings with your fingers, which makes it more difficult to mute the notes immediately after you've played them.

FIGURE 21

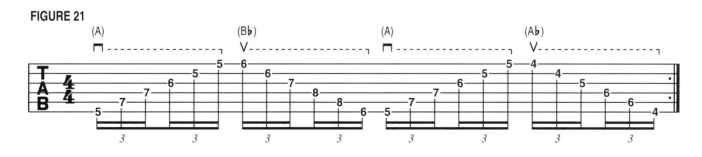

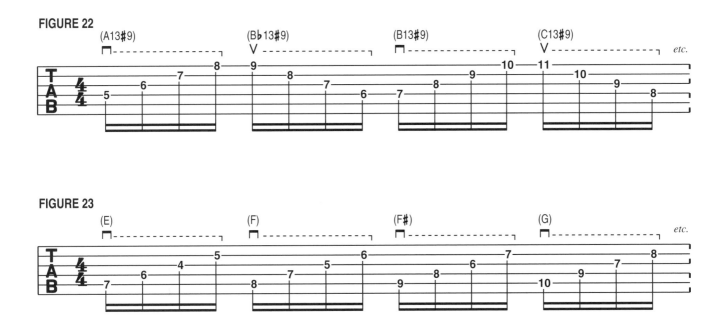

FIGURE 22

FIGURE 23

Multiple Picking

As I mentioned earlier, the best way to develop superhuman chops is to find things that are difficult and even awkward to play and then perform them slowly and perfectly. As an exercise, try playing any given lick or phrase first by alternate picking, then using only downstrokes and, last, using only upstrokes.

You can also devise your own drills where you do any of the following:

- Double picking (picking each note twice)

- Triple pick (… three times)

- Quadruple picking (… four times)

- Quintuple picking (… five times)

HOURS 2, 12, AND 22: SCALES

Practicing scales has many benefits, but the main focus of this activity should be on memorizing the **sound** of a scale and the mood or atmosphere it creates.

Sing the notes you play to help internalize the tonality of the scale, and try to paint a mental picture of what the scale's tonality sounds like to you. This is one of the things you might draw upon when you go to write or improvise music. Beware, however, that when the time comes to take an improvised solo and all you do is flail up and down a scale pattern because you know the notes will work with the chord, you'll most likely sound like a person that knows the fingerings to a particular scale and not an inspired musician.

Learn and play as many scales as you can—in every key and position—in one octave, two octaves, or three octaves. Start from any note on the low E string, then the A string, etc. Make sure you play each scale forward and backward (ascending and descending).

FIGURE 24 illustrates fretboard patterns for the G major scale (G A B C D E F♯) and its **seven relative modes**, all of which comprise the same seven notes. The only difference in each case is the orientation of the notes around a different tonal center, or root.

FIGURE 24 The seven modes of the G major scale (G A B C D E F♯)

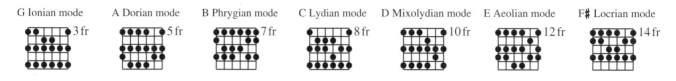

Practice any given scale/mode slowly at first and make sure it's perfect. If you make a mistake, start over. Gradually increase the tempo as you complete a cycle. Listen carefully to each note and focus on *tone*. Before moving to a faster speed, you should be able to run a scale up and down without fudging and notes. Don't cheat yourself! I find it beneficial to watch my fingers in the mirror and try to get them to move gracefully, elegantly, effortlessly, or in whatever way looks and feels good.

There are many things you can do with a scale and mode other than just run it across the fretboard. For example, you can play it in intervals, either melodically, as demonstrated in **FIGURES 25–27**, or up and down the neck on two strings at the same time, as depicted in **FIGURES 28–30**. These first three exercises are great for building technique in both hands, while the second three help you learn the scale on each string and gain *ear-training wisdom* by hearing it played in harmony. To get twice the mileage out of these patterns, be sure to run them in reverse order as well.

FIGURE 25 G major scale in thirds

FIGURE 26 G major scale in fourths

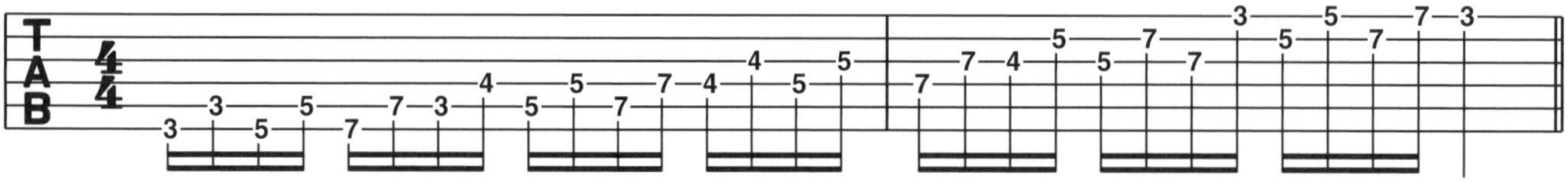

FIGURE 27 G major scale in fifths

FIGURE 28 G major scale in thirds up the neck

FIGURE 29 G major scale in fourths up the neck

FIGURE 30 G major scale in fifths up the neck

There are countless variations on these kinds of melodic and harmonic interval patterns that you can practice. For example, you could take the pattern of ascending diatonic fifths from **FIGURE 27** and switch the order of every other pair of notes to create a different and more interesting melodic contour, as demonstrated in **FIGURE 31**. Considering all the different scales, modes, keys, positions, intervals, and melodic patterns, the possibilities are immense.

FIGURE 31 G major scale in fifths w/melodic variation

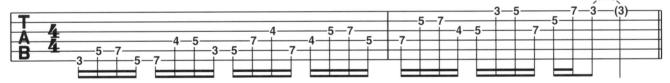

It's also helpful to record yourself practicing scales and then listen critically to your efforts. This will enable you to mold your playing into the direction you want. (I never wanted to sound too polished, and I actually worked on trying to sound gritty and on-the-edge.)

This is obviously a lot to think about when practicing a simple scale, but you don't have to do it all at once. Focus on different elements individually. Eventually they will merge and become part of your second nature.

Pentatonic and Blues Scales

The five-note *minor pentatonic scale* and its derivative, the six-note *minor blues scale*, form the foundation of the vocabulary of rock lead guitar playing. The minor pentatonic scale is spelled "root, minor 3, 4, 5, minor 7." The minor blues scale is made up of these same five notes, plus the diminished or "flatted" fifth ("root, minor 3, 4, flat 5, 5, minor 7"). **FIGURES 32** and **33** illustrate, in the key of E minor, the standard "box" patterns for these two scales that every rock guitarist should know.

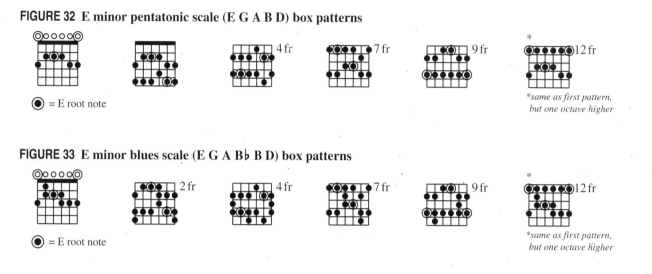

FIGURE 32 E minor pentatonic scale (E G A B D) box patterns

4 fr 7 fr 9 fr * 12 fr

◉ = E root note

*same as first pattern, but one octave higher

FIGURE 33 E minor blues scale (E G A B♭ B D) box patterns

2 fr 4 fr 7 fr 9 fr * 12 fr

◉ = E root note

*same as first pattern, but one octave higher

The minor pentatonic scale and the minor blues scale have a *relative major* that comprises the same set of notes; the only difference is that the notes are oriented around a different root. In each case, the second note of the scale, the minor third, becomes the new root note; in **FIGURES 32** and **33**, this new root note would be G. When played over a G bass note, the E minor pentatonic scale becomes the G major pentatonic scale (G A B D E). Likewise, the E minor blues scale becomes the G major blues scale (G A B♭ B D E) when played over a G bass note.

Try putting the minor and major pentatonic and blues scales through the same paces as the G major scale we looked at earlier by playing them in various interval patterns across the fretboard and up and down the neck.

Other Scales

A scale can contain from two to 12 notes, with the 12-tone *chromatic scale* encompassing every note within an octave. There are numerous scales to choose from, and each has a distinctive sound and color. I have a blast with scale reference books. Some people enjoy first-class trips to Tahiti, but just give me a good scale and I'm in paradise. (How pathetic is that!) But seriously, the reason I'm so intrigued by scales is that the unique tonality of any given scale has the power to transport me.

A couple of years ago I decided to record a live album of compositions I wrote and performed with my band in different parts of the world. As I began this endeavor, which culminated in my CD *Alive in an Ultra World*, I set out to compose material reminiscent of music indigenous to the cultures of the countries I would be visiting. As part of my research, I studied the folk music of each country and figured out the scale(s) upon which much of the native music was based. I then used the scales to compose a set of original pieces. While

I based these compositions on individual scales, I took great pains not to meander up and down the scale aimlessly in my melodies and improvisations. Instead, I emphasized the aura and flavor of the scales within the melody and the chords.

Synthetic Scales

A synthetic scale is one you make up or that does not fall into a particular defined category. For instance, I could make up a scale that contains four notes and is spelled 1, 4, flat 5, 7. I have never seen this scale, but it may have a name already. Whatever the case, I could build chords on this scale, create a melody and figure out how to improvise a solo with it. Furthermore, I could modulate it to different keys and create harmonic textures by using the modes from this scale. Ultimately, if I were to stay within the parameters of the notes of this scale, I guarantee it would create a unique aura.

The more well-known "other" scales include the melodic minor, harmonic minor, whole tone, diminished, and augmented scales. Get a good scale book and have a party!

HOURS 3, 13, AND 23: CHORDS

I've divided chord practice into three areas:

1. Memorization
2. Strumming techniques
3. Improvising

You can dedicate 20 minutes to each category for all three days of the workout, or just focus on one different category for an hour each day.

Memorization

Learn chords! Go buy a book that has all the basic chords as well as all the weird ones. Then, set a goal. For instance, decide you'll learn and memorize five new chords a day. Listen closely and thoughtfully to the sound of a chord as you play the notes it comprises, and try to picture an image that it evokes. Take your time and memorize its sound.

Learn a type of *chord quality*—such as major, minor, major seven, dominant seven, minor seven—in as many positions and voicings as you possibly can. Sing the notes as you play them to help internalize the sound of the chord. Figure out and understand why a chord is called what it's called. What scale degrees does the chord contain? You will need to understand chord theory for this. (That will come later in the "theory" section.)

In addition, strum chords cleanly, gently, harshly, tenderly, brutally, and so on, to get a sense of how they sound with every possible style of playing.

You don't need to know a ton of chords by name in order to be a great musician or songwriter. I have heard that people like Jeff Beck, Allan Holdsworth, and many others may not be familiar with the names or the theory behind all the chords they play, but they have such tremendous ears that, upon hearing a chord, their mind opens up and they know just what to do on their guitars. I happen to find great satisfaction in having a complete understanding of the theory behind it all. Then again, I've always wanted it all.

Strumming

There are many strumming techniques, and numerous books and records can be used for study or as reference sources for these techniques. The most important thing to keep in mind when strumming is to *groove*! After you've chosen a particular strumming pattern to work on, practice it endlessly with a drum machine or a drummer. At first, it will be a little awkward and sloppy. Focus on making it cleaner with every strum; it will get better.

Next, listen carefully to the groove and try to stay locked in with it. You will not be able to groove or lock in with the beat unless you can play the material cleanly or without thinking about the changes. In addition, you must be able to separate yourself a bit from what you're doing and just listen to the beat. By doing this while you're playing, you can really focus on locking in with a drummer. Once you're locked in, keep trying to lock tighter and tighter.

You'll know when you're locked in with the groove because it will start to feel really good. Once you get to this point, you can then experiment by making the groove sound stiff and mechanical, and loose and warm. You can also try to play in front of the beat, behind the beat, and so on.

When you're playing along with a metronome or a drum machine, try to "bury" the click track. By this I mean get right on the beat; when you do, the click will sound as if it's disappeared, since your attacks will be so "right on" that they'll cover the clicks. Being able to lock with the beat and groove is one of the most rewarding feelings one can experience as a musician. It's better than the party after the show… unless, of course, your after-show party is a jam session.

There are many types of grooves to fool around with (straight rock, R&B, reggae, ska, blues shuffle, and so on), but before you do, make sure you can get through them cleanly and lock onto them. Play each across a full range of tempos, from very slow to very fast.

Improvisation/Experimentation

It's always cool to create your own unique chord library. The following are some techniques that can help:

- Play a conventional or familiar chord, then start alternating one note at a time by moving it up or down a fret. When you come across a chord you like, add it to your personal chord library.

- Take numbers from a series (a telephone number, for instance) and use them as scale degrees for a chord.

- Think of an emotion, a color, or a scene from a movie and fool around with the notes in a chord until it sounds like what you're thinking of.

- Use open strings, wide finger stretches, natural harmonics, notes fretted with the fingers on the picking hand, and so on. Experiment with all of these things to come up with unique chords.

HOURS 4, 14, AND 24: EAR TRAINING

If you toss aside everything else in this workout, keep this section. Training your ears is the most important practice in making the crucial connection between your imagination and your fingers. Most people spend very little time developing their ears, but the payoffs from doing so are extraordinary. Some people are born with a natural ear for music, while others need to work on it. It can be tedious and time consuming, but it's very rewarding. The following are some exercises for training your ears.

- Improvise and sing what you play. A good voice isn't necessary, but you do need to get the pitches accurate. If you can't sing the notes perfectly in pitch, work on it until you can.

- Sing a note and then try to play it by using the previous note as a reference. This is a challenging drill that takes a tremendous amount of discipline. Just imagine, though, how much your ears will improve when you can do this.

- Sing a harmony to notes you're playing. Start with something simple, like a fifth, then move to a fourth, a major third, a minor third, a major sixth, and so on, until you're able to sing a harmony part (like a minor second) perfectly to an improvised atonal solo. Understand that this ability could take years to develop.

- Memorize the sound of different intervals. One way to do this is to record yourself playing an interval and, after a few seconds of silence, speaking its name. Fill up a one-hour tape, then listen back and try to name each interval in the silence that follows the notes. You'll know if you're right when your voice comes in and names it properly.

- Perform this last exercise with chords. Record yourself slowly plucking each note of a chord, and allow a few seconds of space between the notes. After a moment of silence, announce the chord and its component intervals.

- Transcribe everything, from simple guitar solos to complex jazz sax solos.

- Carry manuscript paper with you, and when you have some free time away from your instrument, write melodies using only your ears to guide you.

- Carry songbooks with you and sing the melodies.

- Make up your own ear training exercises and keep a log of your progress.

HOURS 5, 15, AND 25: READING MUSIC

There are a lot of advantages to reading music. Some of the perks include:

- Learning to play songs you otherwise wouldn't have been able to play

- Being able to transcribe your compositions

- Expanding your musical palate

When I was a student at Berklee College of Music in Boston, I decided I wanted to be the best sight-reader in the world. I spent an entire summer doing nothing but sight-reading almost every waking moment. I remember leaving the apartment only two times for social events the entire summer. I attempted to sight-read everything I could get my hands on—clarinet studies, piano pieces, John Coltrane sax solos, Joe Pass chord charts, and even phone books. At the end of the summer I was a mediocre sight-reader at best.

I believe the guitar is the most difficult instrument on which to sight-read because there are limitations and many variables involved. Having said that, I can provide some pointers.

The two most important elements in learning to read music well are being able to identify patterns and to look ahead as you're playing. Work on these principles and things will eventually fall into place. Beyond these tips, I recommend you do the following:

- Buy beginner guitar books to get the idea of where the notes fall on the instrument. I have never been a big fan of reading guitar tab, probably because I always preferred the little black dots. But for a guitarist, tab is an excellent way to get a bird's-eye overview of how to play a particular piece.

- Take a song (classical, jazz, or whatever you like) and read it through every day until you can play it perfectly. Sight-reading is really about identifying patterns, so this will help. Once you have completely mastered a song and you're capable of playing it flawlessly without having to think where your fingers need to go, go ahead and play it many more times and watch what happens. Your ability to make an emotional investment in what you are playing will arise. This is when what you're playing will start to sound like music and not just something your fingers know how to play.

- Build a repertoire of songs and play through each one every day, or on a regular basis at least.

- Sight-read a little bit of something new and terrifying every day. This will aid your ability to look ahead.

It's been proven that the most effective way to improve your sight-reading ability is to attempt to sight-read something at a strict tempo, such as with a metronome or drum machine. The key is to proceed without stopping or slowing down. If you miss a note, oh well. Keep going, as if you were giving a recital with other musicians. Don't stop and dwell on the note(s) you missed until you've finished the entire piece, then go back and see what you missed. Practice sight-reading a piece of music you're working on at a tempo that's not going to make you mess up every two measures. You'll be amazed at how your sight-reading ability will improve by forcing yourself not to slow down when you come to a tricky spot.

In addition, read music for instruments other than guitar, such as the clarinet, flute, and piano. Also, get a jazz "fake" book and read through the chord changes.

HOURS 6, 16, AND 26: WRITING MUSIC

Writing songs or instrumental pieces is one of the most rewarding things about being a musician. There are many ways you can go about building a catalog of original material. When I was a high school freshman I had an incredible music theory teacher named Bill Westcott. He was tough! One of my assignments was to come in every day with a newly written piece of original music that he could play on the piano. It had to be completely notated and not just show chord symbols and melody, and it had to be written specifically for the piano. Having him play the music for me was not only a treat but tremendously educational.

If you're interested in learning how to notate music properly, the best reference book on the subject is *Music Notation* by Gardner Read. It's an exceptional book, and it outlines all the essential "do's" and "don'ts." You may be able to find it by calling the bookstore at Berklee College of Music in Boston.

Here are some recommendations for songwriting/composing:

- Turn on a tape recorder and bang out your idea. I can't tell you how important this is if you want to be a songwriter. Moments of inspiration are sometimes few and far between, and they can hit you at the most unlikely times. You need to be ready to capture them when they present themselves.

- Write songs out in lead sheet format, with a melody on the staff and chord changes written above the melody. There are books, such as *Music Notation*, that outline the limitations and proper notation for various instruments in the orchestra as well as more unconventional instruments. Get some manuscript or score paper and try composing music for instruments other than the guitar. Study the range, tone, timbre, limitations, and notation for one instrument at a time, be it violin, harp, or harmonica played through a Marshall stack (or a Carvin Legacy stack).

- Find another musician that you can "gel with" as a cowriter. Ideally, he or she may be someone who possesses certain skills that you're lacking. If you have the right chemistry, creating music with another person can be a very rewarding experience.

- While lying in bed at night, try to make up an endless melody that contains a variety of instruments. Doing this is truly liberating, because you're creating instantaneously, and there are no limitations to where you can go or what it can sound like.

Remember that people write songs based on anything from events in their life to social commentary to fantasy. When a person taps into that creative portion of their brain, they usually gravitate to things that stimulate them the most.

HOURS 7, 17, AND 27: MUSIC THEORY

I've always been fascinated by music theory. Although knowledge of it is not a prerequisite for being a great guitar player or musician, I feel that if you're going to learn to speak a language, it helps if you know how to read and write it. Many people are intimidated by theory, but it's not that difficult, really; the system is actually very logical and straightforward. What confuses a lot of people, I think, is having to struggle with thinking in unfamiliar keys, such as A flat or F sharp.

Bill Westcott taught me music theory in high school, but it wasn't until I took guitar lessons from Joe Satriani that I learned how to apply a lot of it to my instrument. There are many books that teach music theory basics, including notation, time signatures, key signatures, the circle of fifths, chord theory, and modes. I recommend that you take everything you learn in a theory book and figure out how it applies to the guitar and how you can incorporate it into your own style.

HOURS 8–10, 18–20, 28–30: JAMMING

In this section, I'll explain methods to help you find your unique voice as a guitarist and explain techniques that can aid your expression on the instrument. These latter items include vibrato, bent notes, harmonics, whammy bar stunts, and dynamics.

Everything I've told you thus far will help you in your quest to become an accomplished guitar player. However, all the exercises, scales, theory, and whatnot are just devices that can help you express yourself more freely on your instrument. Be careful not to get hung up on how fascinating it is to be able to play scales really fast, or to shred yourself into a coma. Use this stuff as a tool, not a prison. Sitting and playing the instrument expressively and with control is the goal here. These days, I don't practice all of the material I've mentioned, but it has all been crucial to my development and to making my ears, fingers, and soul work together in expressing the music I have in my head.

I believe that we all have the ability to be unique on our instruments. The trick is being able to identify with that uniqueness and then cultivate it into a stimulating presentation (or maybe even a historical statement). I have found that listening to my inner ear is the best way to get to the heart of the matter. It's a sometimes subtle, elusive voice, but it's there, and there are concrete ways to tune into it.

When I sit down to play now, I usually build "jam tracks" to improvise over and write to. There are numerous ways you can do this. One way is to learn the basics of home recording and invest in a simple rig with which you can record your own tracks to jam over. You can also purchase prerecorded jam tracks on CD, and some electronic devices—like Korg's Pandora—feature built-in vamps you can play with. (I never travel without my Pandora.)

Focusing intensely on anything is a form of meditation and, as such, it has the potential to increase IQ, comprehension, imagination, and artistic abilities at any age. The problem is that it's difficult for many of us (including yours truly) to keep the mind focused on anything for a long period of time. This, however, is the only way to get real results. You need to meditate on what you're doing, and when the mind begins to wander, you need to try to pull it back.

To that end, I'd like to present various techniques for you to practice while jamming with a tape or a band, or just sitting in your room. First, however, I would like to make the following suggestions:

- Use a variety of loops that encompass different genres, grooves, keys, and time signatures. By setting up specific parameters (whether stylistic, melodic, or rhythmic in nature), you'll push yourself to discover different ways of approaching various techniques. This will help you identify who you really are on the instrument because you'll be forced to reach deep inside yourself and find the things that push your musical buttons.

- When doing any of the following technique exercises, use them to express the way various emotions feel to you: anger, joy, lust, compassion, melancholy, paranoia, euphoria—whatever. Each of these emotions has an audible counterpart. Beware, however, that to successfully transmit these emotions from your psyche to your fingers, you will need to immerse yourself in the emotion itself. The way to do this is to think thoughts that are in line with the kind of emotion you are trying to conjure up. The way we feel is a reflection of the thoughts we choose to think. Our emotions follow our thoughts. Some may believe that it's the other way around, but it's not. If you feel compelled to focus more on angry or negative thoughts, then those corresponding emotions will arise in you and whatever you create will carry the energy of that emotion. I recommend trying to keep things balanced—after all, you are what you play, and wherever your thoughts go they will inevitably shape your attitude and perspective on life. Whatever thoughts you think will attract like-minded thoughts and will perpetuate your frame of mind and emotional equilibrium. Keep this in mind as it has 100% to do with the art you create and the quality of life you will live. It's easy to be miserable and intense, but it can be a challenge to unearth negative mind patterns and turn them into positive ones. Now that you understand this, this exercise can help you to imagine and bring to reality the kind of musician and person you would like to be.

- It's also helpful when you find yourself in a particular funk (due to the ups and downs of life), because it can help strengthen the mental tools you may need to pull yourself in a particular direction.

- Record yourself playing, then listen back to identify the cool, interesting stuff that's mixed in alongside the more conventional and perhaps uninspired things. The minute you hear yourself doing something different or interesting, take whatever that is and make an exercise out of it. Continue to pull yourself in this new direction that accentuates your uniqueness. It's like finding a little thread and pulling it into enough material to knit a sweater... or a whole wardrobe, for that matter!

With all this in mind, following are some techniques to focus on.

Vibrato

I have always thought of vibrato as the soul of a note. There are myriad vibratos that can be used as tools to express your ideas.

Try fretting a note with your index finger and hold it for a few minutes while effecting a vibrato that morphs from extremely slow to fast to violent and brutal. Make sure your intonation is good or you'll sound like a hack. Try different oscillations, from a subtle rise and fall in pitch to a very wide modulation, and don't let your finger slip off the string. Exaggerate all of your actions.

Now do the same thing with each finger of your fretting hand.

Next, hold two notes at a time and shake them in a similar manner. Then try doing this with three notes, then four, and so on.

Apply vibrato to a note that you've already bent upward a half step, a whole step, or two whole steps. Many players feel they can be more expressive with vibrato by applying it to a note that's already bent, for the simple reason that it can go below the main pitch as well as above it.

Try doing this with every finger on every fret of the guitar. Doing so will teach you to take a different approach and grip to apply vibrato to notes on different strings in different areas of the fretboard. You'll find that as you move away from the 12th fret (the midpoint between your guitar's bridge and nut), the strings feel stiffer and are harder to wiggle.

Bending Notes

Bending strings well is an art unto itself, one that requires a high degree of aural and tactile sensitivity, mental and physical discipline, and technical control over your instrument. Few things sound worse than a guitar player that has no control over his pitch when bending notes; it's as if someone is singing off-key. Yet, when executed well, a bent note on the guitar is one of the most musically expressive sounds, one that enraptures the listener and causes goose bumps. A bent note just has so much more attitude and feeling than its unbent counterpart.

Sit for an hour and do nothing but bend notes. Bend them up as far as you like, but make sure you zero in on the "target note" that you want to hit. Listen carefully and critically to your pitch and strive for impeccable intonation. (This is comparable to what a violinist, singer, trombonist, or slide guitar player must do all the time.)

Practicing *unison bends* is an effective way to train your fingers and ears to work together to bend in tune. To play a unison bend, fret a note on the B string with your index finger while placing your ring finger on the G string two frets higher. Strum both strings together, then quickly push the G string note away from your palm to raise its pitch up a whole step so that it perfectly matches the pitch of the unbent note on the B string.

In addition:

- Try bending two strings at the same time (double-stop bending).
- Start with a note in a bent position and bring it either down or up, or up and then down. Push yourself to try different things.
- Play bent notes together with unbent notes on different strings. This is a very slick country guitar technique that developed out of a desire by players to emulate the weeping sound of the pedal steel.
- Make sure to practice bending as much in the upper register and on the high strings as you do in the lower register and on the low strings. Can you bend an F# note at the second fret on the high E string up to A? Maybe if you're Zakk Wylde!

Harmonics

Do nothing but focus on playing harmonics for an hour. Experiment with different types and techniques, including the following:

- Play open-string, or "natural," harmonics by lightly touching any string with your fretting hand at various points along the string and picking it.
- Sound "artificial" harmonics by fretting a note with the left hand and picking the string with a downstroke while also "pinching" it between the pick and right thumb. Move the pick along the string in the area over the pickups as you do this to find various "sweet spots."
- Try tapping notes over certain frets while fretting a note.
- Be adventurous and try to discover different techniques for sounding harmonics. (Playing with distortion and with your guitar's bridge pickup on helps bring out harmonics.)

Whammy Bar Stunts

The whammy bar is my favorite "crutch." If your guitar's whammy bar is set up anything like mine, you can pull up on it to make notes go sharp as well as push down on it to make notes turn into sheer blubber. I can abuse the hell out of my whammy bar and it usually comes right back in tune. The setup is very important. Try the following experiments:

- Play melodies by fingering only one note and using the whammy bar to raise and lower its pitch.
- Play various kinds of harmonics and experiment with pulling and pushing the whammy to produce "outer space" sounds.
- Try to create everything from nice, subtle vibrato on single notes and full chords to violent sonic brutality and sheer warbling cacophony. (I seem to have made a career out of doing this.)

I could go on forever, but I encourage you to create your own techniques. Your only real guideline here is to do whammy bar things exclusively for a long period of time without stopping. Sooner or later you'll come across little treasures.

Dynamics

One of the things that make the guitar such an expressive instrument is its wide dynamic (volume) range. Few people utilize the full dynamic range of the instrument. You can hit the thing extremely hard and forcefully, and then immediately switch to a style that is caressing and tender. Not many players can do both of these things effectively in the period of three seconds, so try to become one of the few who can. Here are a few ways to practice:

- Gradually go from soft to hard, and then back again.

- Create a strumming pattern that has sharp hits, light strums, and medium rhythmic things all in one or two bars.

- Play as loud and as hard as you possibly can without stopping for as long as you're able to. Then do the exact opposite.

Again, I could go on forever, but I think you get the point.

To close out this section on jamming, I've pulled together a number of ways you can set up parameters to force you into making new discoveries on the guitar. Try to do each of the following for an hour without stopping:

- Solo on one string only.

- Solo with double-stops only (two notes played together), then try doing the same thing with three-, four-, five-, and six-note chords.

- Solo on two adjacent strings only, then solo on two strings that have one, two, three, or four idle strings between them.

- Record a vamp that has a single bass note repeating under it, then improvise over the vamp while limiting yourself to one particular mode or synthetic scale.

- Play a chord, listen to it, then close your eyes and imagine a scene that the chord evokes. This can be done with a melody line, too.

- Pick one note and play it as many different ways as you can for an hour. Make it sound like music.

- Come up with at least one new thing a day that you've never played before.

- Improvise with only one hand (your fretting hand), using only hammer-ons and pull-offs to articulate notes. Make sure the notes sound good and clear, and not sloppy.

- Play as fast and as cleanly as you can without stopping.

- Play as slowly and tenderly as you can.

- Try fooling around with alternate tunings. Include radically different tunings that seem to make no sense.

- Try to evoke colors with chords.

- Lay your guitar on the floor and touch it in many different ways, trying to create unique sounds.

HOURS 31–40: REST

Don't hurt yourself. If you need to take a break, then take one. You needn't feel guilty if you miss a practice session. (Well, maybe a little guilty.) When you're young and have time to kill, without all the pressures and responsibilities that saddle you later on, it's easier to put in the hours.

Keep in mind that your fingers have many tiny and intricate muscles that, like any other muscle, need rest to recuperate and heal after a workout. Evaluate your own pain threshold, and don't be afraid to rest if your fingers really feel like they need it. Few of us practice for 10 hours a day, and you should give yourself ample time to achieve the stamina to play for such a long period of time.

I seem to have been blessed with great finger genes. My fingers are long and nimble, and they can take tremendous abuse. Back when I was putting in many hours of practicing, I could go for 15 to 20 hours at a stretch, without any wrist, finger, or forearm pain. A little muscle fatigue was about all I experienced. On the occasions that I felt pain, I just worked through it. Today, however, *I do not recommend this!* I encourage every guitarist reading this workout to be on the alert for signs of common musician ailments, such as tendonitis and carpal tunnel syndrome. They can be very dangerous if not addressed.

Two last notes on the subject. First, if you want to keep your calluses on your fingertips, then you need to protect your hands from getting wet for any long period of time. Second, protect your ears more cautiously than your penis. If you're doing loud gigs, put cotton or earplugs in them. (This may be the best advice you get from this article!)

PLAY WITH OTHERS

If you get anything out of this piece, it should be this: share the experience of making music with others. If that's all you do, you're doing pretty good.

I have not incorporated this concept into the body of the 30-hour cycle, but for me it's the most rewarding aspect of being a musician. Making music, like making love, can be a very sharing, tender, touchy-feely, emotional experience. It can also be a sheer expression of other things.

My favorite types of musicians to play with are those who know how to *listen* and *interact* accordingly. To communicate musically, you must have the ability to allow others into your expressive psyche. To really let others in can be an intimate experience. By the same token, you need to have the ability to listen to others around you and interact accordingly. Mutual respect and a nonjudgmental attitude are some of the elements necessary in cultivating the right chemistry to make that magic.

Some of my favorite times in my life are the years that I attended Berklee. I learned a lot about myself during that period. The school was filled with young, budding, ambitious musicians, and the group of students I hung out with became much like family. There were different musicians from all around the world there, playing all sorts of instruments, and they were eager to explore, share, and communicate through music. Nothing can beat that kind of attitude and those kinds of moments, no matter how many hours you spend practicing in your room. There were some tremendous players there, and I bonded with people who have become lifelong friends.

When I was in high school, I was in a band called Rayge, and we played cover tunes by Led Zeppelin, Kiss, Queen, Deep Purple, and others. We eventually started to do a lot of original music as well. Our attitude in those days was one of brotherhood. We went through many life experiences together, but the most important thing was the band. None of us were selfish about sharing music when we hit the rehearsal basement or the stage. We went through many "coming of age" experiences together, and at times those experiences were joyous, and at other times tragic. Regardless, we always had the band and each other.

What I'm getting at here is how important it is to play selflessly with others. Doing so will give you the opportunity to respect others, experiment, open your ears, react and, of course, throw up on the gym floor after the gig at the high school dance.

DISCOVERING YOURSELF

This workout and approach may be highly criticized in the future for being "over the top," but I personally don't know of any other way to become a virtuoso but to work really hard at it with great passion. This is not a class on being a great musician or songwriting (although it may help in those areas), but a celebration of the guitar and your own potential with it.

The commitment it takes to become an elite virtuoso guitarist is not unlike that required to become a champion in any other field. You must think, breathe, eat, and live the instrument at virtually every waking moment (and even while sleeping, when possible). You must transcend the games your mind will play on you and the excuses it will give you to lay off and take the easy road. Frankly, none of these excuses come up for those who are truly passionate about being the best they can be. You must continually bring the focus back to the instrument. You may find yourself being harshly criticized by other music community people, or friends, magazines, and those that hang around on Sunset Boulevard obsessing over the nuances of the latest trends. This is precisely the time when you need to fearlessly stick to your vision. There are tests all along the way. Realize it's all in the mind, and never accept anything less than the best you can do when dealing with things that are within your ability to control.

Keep a positive outlook on things and watch that your accomplishments and intensity don't turn you into a self-centered, ego-maniacal prick. Always compliment and support your fellow musicians. We all have dreams and hopes. By encouraging, sincerely complimenting and supporting those around us, we gain self-dignity, respect, friends, a healthy overview of our own work, and an appreciation for the efforts that others put in during their struggles.

It's OK to get discouraged at times, but it's not OK to quit. Quitting is never an option for a true artist. It's just not in their makeup and would rarely even cross their mind. Think of music and the guitar when you're not even around an instrument. If you're in a quiet setting, imagine that you're playing and try to see your fingers moving while you listen to what's happening in your head. You can get better at this as time goes by. It's unbelievably rewarding and it can help you improve drastically because you're not confined by your physical limitations. I used to do this all the time, and I still do. I imagine things on the instrument that I can't do, and then I work on them until I can do them effortlessly.

If you see me as an example of a current-day, conventional-type guitar virtuoso, then use my accomplishments as something to rise above. That's one way in which evolution works. When you see what's possible in a field you are interested in, it enables you to create a goal that adds to it. It's inevitable that this will happen. Why not make it you who does it? There are many ways to add to what exists without being competitive. There is plenty of success to go around. It's actually infinite.

If you find yourself feeling uninspired about all this, it's OK to admit to yourself that perhaps you don't really want to be a virtuoso. That's totally OK. You can still enjoy playing the guitar at your own pace and leisure for the rest of your life without any pressure. But a true virtuoso has no choice. Playing the guitar is akin to the air they breathe. But it would be worse to beat yourself up for not wanting to be something that your ego may be telling you that you should be. Look for feeling fulfilled by just touching the instrument and enjoying whatever comes out as a gift.

There are those who believe that everything in the physical Universe, and other dimensions, is a manifestation of God, or pure consciousness. And that everything we do, especially when we are being creative, is God's way of expanding the Universe through us. I am not an authority on these things, but it seems to me (and to most physicists) that everything in the creation has a vibration to it, so in some respects you can say that everything is music. We may not be able to hear it with our physical ears, but it resonates within all of us. Could this be why we are so fond of music? Creating music just by "willing" it in your head may eventually lead to just listening to it happen in your head. Who the composer is and where the music takes you are for each individual to discover.

DISCLAIMER

I do not claim to have the control over the mind as is entirely outlined through this lesson. At this time I'm still a work in progress. I talk the talk so I can find a path to try and walk the walk.

Some people have an abundance of natural talent and are more gifted in some areas than others. I always felt that I was naturally gifted musically because I heard music, and saw it in my head, for as long as I can remember. But I don't believe I was naturally gifted as a guitar player; I had to work very hard to develop my chops and techniques. I know lots of players that are better shredders, cleaner players, and better sight-readers than I am. And I always felt that if most people put in the time that I put in, they would probably have a superior technique to mine. I'm not trying to be self-deprecating either. I've had students that showed an extraordinary ability to develop amazing technique in a relatively short period of time, but may have had redundant, dull ideas. Conversely, I've had students that found it very difficult to play anything accurately, but their ideas and sense of melody were inspired. And then there are those freaks that have it all.

I think being a musician and being able to play an instrument is about the coolest thing in the world. Creating music (and especially playing the guitar) is most rewarding when it's based on pure passion. It's our birthright to play an instrument and to create.

Of course, you can toss the whole concept of this article and just do it your own way. However, some things won't change. The amount of focus, passion, and time you put in are going to be reflected in your results. Whatever the case, there really are no rules. My best suggestion would be to find the thing that is most exciting to you about the guitar and just throw yourself into it and to quote Frank Zappa, "There are only two things to remember. Number one, don't stop and number two, keep going."

OTHER STEVE VAI BOOKS AND DVD AT HAL LEONARD

BOOKS

Alien Love Secrets	Guitar Recorded Versions	00690039	$24.95
Alien Love Secrets: Naked Vamps	Signature Licks	00695223	$22.95
Alive in an Ultra World	Guitar Recorded Versions	00690575	$22.95
Fire Garden	Guitar Recorded Versions	00690172	$24.95
Fire Garden: Naked Vamps	Signature Licks	00695166	$22.95
Flex-Able Leftovers	Guitar Recorded Versions	00690343	$19.95
Passion & Warfare	Guitar Recorded Versions	00660137	$24.95
Real Illusions: Reflections	Guitar Recorded Versions	00690881	$24.95
The Elusive Light and Sound, Vol. 1	Guitar Recorded Versions	00690605	$24.95
Sex & Religion	Guitar Recorded Versions	00694904	$24.95
Steve Vai Guitar Styles & Techniques	Signature Licks	00673247	$22.95
The Story of Light	Guitar Recorded Versions	00110385	$22.99
The Ultra Zone	Guitar Recorded Versions	00690392	$19.95
The Ultra Zone: Naked Vamps	Signature Licks	00695684	$22.95

DVD

Alien Love Secrets		00320540	$19.95